Goodreads

Entrepreneurs

Social Networking for the Creative Mind

Lisa Shea

TABLE OF CONTENTS

Seize the Day

INTRODUCTION

Goodreads. Even the name is friendly. Good Reads. Things that are good to read. It brings to mind a warm, supportive community of book readers.

Goodreads used to be a wholly independent website made up of people who loved books. It was launched in 2006. Then in 2013, Amazon bought it. It's no surprise why Amazon was interested in a book review site with over 20 million members. For authors, that means this site is a huge opportunity for building a fan base

This book will show you how.

I have run my own company since 1999. My websites have been amongst the top of the internet. I have written over 300 books. I have won awards with my photography and other artwork. My origami was featured on a Today show wedding. I have years of experience in the worlds of running a business, writing for a living, and selling artwork.

My Goodreads page is absolutely an active one. This is one of the most critical places for authors to hang out. Even if you're not an author, this site lets you reach millions of users in a supportive, community environment.

Let my experiences guide you through the ins and outs of Goodreads. With the help of my quick, easy, step by step instructions, you'll soon be using Goodreads to sell your books, spread the word about your projects, and reach whatever other goals you have!

The way to start is to take that first step.

I support local children's art programs.

Note: If you also have my Facebook book (or one of my other social networking books), you'll find that certain categories of this information overlaps. For example, the theory behind high quality eye-catching image design is fairly standard across the web. I aim to keep those types of sections similar across these books so that a person reading, for example, the Instagram book and then the Goodreads book can see where those two relate. This can help a lot with cross-posting activities.

My aim is that, by reading this book, you'll be learning a foundation which you can then apply to many other social networking projects.

CHAPTER 1 – THE BASICS

Goodreads is a site primarily focused on book reviews and book promotions. That being said, it can be useful for entrepreneurs of all backgrounds.

Goodreads was launched in 2006 and currently has over 20 million members. Yes, it's not as many as Facebook or Twitter. However, the people who are on Goodreads can be quite fanatical. They can post there all day long. By having your own entries show up in this system, it can guarantee you visibility.

Here's a quick summary of how the Goodreads process works. There are then step-by-step instructions below to help you with each aspect of the process.

You start by going to goodreads.com. You set up an account there. You load up an image of some sort - either your photo or maybe a cute image related to your topic area.

That's it!

Now you make a little post about what you are doing. Maybe you're reading an interesting book in your topic area. Maybe you've just posted a new article on feeding your parakeet. Maybe you're drinking a new wine! You can include a URL in your Goodreads posting, so it's a great way to build traffic to your website or blog.

Once you have your Goodreads feed working properly, you can add a bookmark to your web browser, perhaps in a new folder called "Social Networking." You visit it every day and update your Goodreads page with what you're doing. If you have made a new blog post or other similar content update, be sure to link to that. That way your Goodreads followers get alerts when you've added new content.

Let your friends know about your new Goodreads feed. Mention it in your newsletter and forum! Yes, not all people will be interested in checking out Goodreads - but a lot of people DO use this service. By providing your updates in as many ways as possible, you ensure that as many people know about your information as possibly can. You're covering all the bases. You never know who might enjoy the Goodreads feed and use that as their main method of keeping track of you!

You also never know which Goodreads fans might be randomly searching the Goodreads system, find you, and suddenly learn about your fantastic project. You could get a whole new group of followers who had never heard of you before.

I have heard from countless authors, artists, and bands that their sales drastically increased once they began using Goodreads properly. It is well worth the small time investment to make those posts.

And best of all, it's free!

So let's get started!

IMPORTANT NOTE ON GOODREADS RATINGS

Most people on the web are now used to the Amazon star system. In Amazon, a 1-star means the book sucked. A 5-star means the book was great. A 3-star means the book was barely tolerable.

THIS IS NOT HOW GOODREADS WORKS.

The Goodreads rating system has caused endless grief to authors who don't understand that this is a different scale.

You can hover over any star beneath a book to see how Goodreads is supposed to work.

Yes, that's right, a 3-star means YOU LIKED IT. Sure, a 1-star means you didn't like it, but they assume that once you get to 3 stars you do like the book. You enjoyed it. It just means it's not one of your top-10 favorites.

A 5-star on Goodreads is supposed to mean this is one of your most favorite books of all time that you will re-read and re-read continuously.

That is quite different from what Amazon means from 5-star.

Now that so many people are importing their Amazon reviews into Goodreads, and new users are flooding in who just use Amazon-style rankings for books, the Goodreads system is a mess. There are some people using the "proper" Goodreads rankings. There are many people using the "more star-filled" Amazon ranking. People who are used to one system get confused by the other.

So, in the end, at least try to stay consistent with your own reviews and then use the text description area to explain why you gave the rating you did.

If you're an author and other people are reviewing your books, take a deep breath if you see three stars or even two stars. For some people, especially long-timers on Goodreads, those are good reviews. It means they enjoyed your book.

CHAPTER 2 – CREATING THE ACCOUNT

The very first step in any project is to begin. To start with Goodreads, it's time to create your account.

If you've already created an account, read through here to see if there were any steps you missed.

SIGNING UP FOR GOODREADS

So you're interested in getting started with Goodreads! That's wonderful. Here are the step by step instructions to get you on your way. Note that these Goodreads screenshots were done in May 2017 so they might have changed slightly depending on when you read this. However, Goodreads hasn't changed much since it was launched in 2006 so it's likely that any tiny changes won't impact how you sign up.

To begin with, go to Goodreads.com on your computer or mobile device. People actively use both systems for using Goodreads. Goodreads, of course, makes it incredibly easy to sign up. Just fill in your information. Note that I do NOT recommend auto-signing-up with another account. Keep your accounts separate for security reasons.

Goodreads will encourage you to connect with all your social networking friends. I do recommend doing this – but you don't have to do it right now. It's very easy to do this once you're set up. So it's fine to skip this step for now to save time.

Get book recommendations from your friends!
Check your address book to find friends on Goodreads.

We compare your email address book with all 55
million Goodreads members and show you who is
already on the site. You can also optionally invite
friends that are not yet on the site to compare books
with them.

skip this step »

The "skip this step" is on the right side.

Next up, they'll ask you to set up a reading goal. You can skip this as well if you wish.

Set a Reading Goal!

Join **2,079,981** other readers in the 2017 Goodreads Reading Challenge!
Tell Goodreads how many books you want to read this year, and we'll help you stay on track!

I want to read   #   books in 2017.

Take the Challenge

skip this step »

OK, now they'll ask you for your favorite genre of book. It really doesn't matter at all. Just choose something – anything. Don't stress about it.

Next, select your favorite genres.

We use your favorite genres to make better book recommendations and tailor what you see in your Updates feed.

☐ Art	☐ Biography	☐ Business	☐ Chick Lit	☐ Children's
☐ Christian	☐ Classics	☐ Comics	☐ Contemporary	☐ Cookbooks
☐ Crime	☐ Ebooks	☐ Fantasy	☐ Fiction	☐ Gay and Lesbian
☐ Graphic Novels	☐ Historical Fiction	☐ History	☐ Horror	☐ Humor and Comedy
☐ Manga	☐ Memoir	☐ Music	☐ Mystery	☐ Nonfiction
☐ Paranormal	☐ Philosophy	☐ Poetry	☐ Psychology	☐ Religion
☐ Romance	☐ Science	☐ Science Fiction	☐ Self Help	☐ Suspense
☐ Spirituality	☐ Sports	☐ Thriller	☐ Travel	☐ Young Adult

Don't see your favorite genres here?

Based on the genre you chose, they will now encourage you to rate books. That's what this system was founded on, after all – people rating books. And what's a bit annoying about this is they don't even tell you how the Goodreads rating system works at this point. But in any case, you can ignore the request for now. Just click on the 'I'm finished rating' in the top right corner.

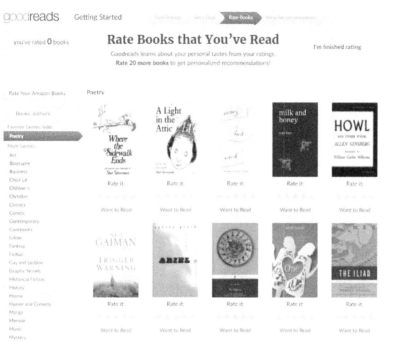

When you don't rate the books, Goodreads will sadly inform you that it can't recommend more books for you to read yet. That's ok. That's not why you're here. Still, take a moment to feel properly sad that Goodreads can't push you to buy yet more books for your library ;).

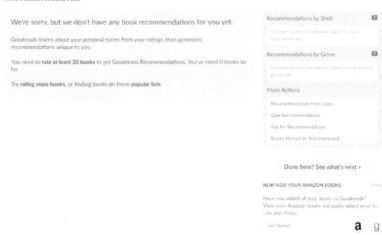

So click on "Done here" on the right side.

Voila. You're at the home screen. It's time to start customizing!

Note that you'll get an email verifying you are who you say you are. Be sure to click that at some point.

HANDLING GOODREADS NOTIFICATIONS

Like most social networks, Goodreads has the potential to hammer you with emails about every single update. It's good to rein that in early. Go to your profile in the top right and click on emails.

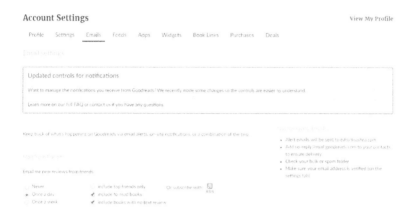

I highly recommend turning this all off. If you want to you can always turn things back on again.

Just unclick everything. There's an "unsubscribe from all" link at the very bottom but I feel a bit more secure doing it manually. Besides, it's good to see what the options are in case you want to turn something back on later.

CHOOSING A PROFILE ICON

A main thing you are doing with Google is expanding the branding of you as a writer, artist, or however you wish to become known. Therefore it's critical that you choose an icon that continues your branding. You change your photo by clicking on "Profile" as the first left-most option on your settings screen. That'll bring you to the area where you set your icon.

Account Settings   View My Profile

Profile   Settings   Emails   Feeds   Apps   Widgets   Book Links   Purchases   Deals

First Name *
Linda

Middle Name

Last Name
DeFeudis

Display Name   Choose File   No file chosen
Linda DeFeudis ▾   Upload Photo

Show my last name to
● Anyone (including search engines!)
○ Friends

User Name

Gender
Select ▾

Gender Viewable By
Friends Only ▾
Note: Pronouns (he, she, they) will be seen by everyone regardless of this setting

Make sure the photo you choose is nearly square and clearly visible at the small size. Many Goodreads users are using Goodreads on their phones. Your photo is going to be the size of a gnat on there. It has to be recognizable at that tiny size. If you want the image to show you as a person, don't show a full body image - show just a close-up on the face.

Make sure the photo is well taken. If the photo is fuzzy or out of focus it is going to give a poor impression to your readers.

People really do care about those sorts of issues. People react very strongly to images.

Remember, your icon shows up next to EVERY POST YOU MAKE. That is a huge amount of promotion. It needs to do a good job.

I would NOT use a stock photo or generic image. Again, this is all about branding. Branding your name and words with a stock photo or image is anti-branding. :) It will do you no good in the long run. People are keyed to visual images and if you are building your reputation as a writer you can use every boost you can get! Definitely use your photo, and make it the best photo you can get. It is far better to use a photo and later upgrade to a "better photo" than to have a generic, meaningless image that will not provide any value to you.

Whatever you do, don't stay with the initial "empty face." The default image for a brand new Goodreads account is a blank face. This is a sign of a spammer and many people automatically block blank-face-accounts. Make sure you replace that blank-face as soon as possible.

It's fine to practice and test different options to see what works best both on PC screens and on smartphones. If you don't have a smartphone, enlist a friend to lend a hand with testing. You need that image to be recognizable and clear.

Once you settle on an image, it's best to stick with it. People will come to associate your image with you as an account. They'll look for that image and when tweets come through their stream they'll recognize it. If you then randomly change your image every week, they'll lose that ability. They will not have as strong a connection with your posts. So while it's good to experiment until you get a great image that works well at small sizes, once you find one, stick with it.

PROFILE CUSTOMIZATION

Most other social networks have top banners, backgrounds, and other things to customize.

Goodreads is not like that.

Your key thing to customize is that profile icon. Once that is set, you're pretty set.

Your main aims now are to:

- add in friends, from your social networks
- review a few books
- make a few posts in various forums

If you're an author, thought, an absolutely key next step is to take control of your author profile.

What you just set up here is a regular user profile. It's what 'typical users' have. As an author, you need to take the next step to lay claim to the books you've written.

So let's take a look at that, if you're an author.

CLAIMING YOUR AUTHOR PROFILE

In Goodreads, everyone logs in as a user. Users can review books and make posts.

But authors can do more than that. Authors can claim their books and make updates about their books. They can gain followers. So it's important for authors to know how to do that

First, you need that regular user profile. So make sure you do that first.

Once you have a profile set up with a profile image, go to the search box on the top of your screen.

Search for your own name, to find your books.

Search

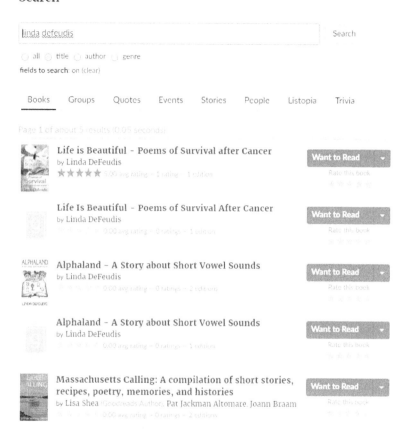

If Amazon is working properly, your books will show up. If it isn't, skip forward to the area about how to add in books manually. But for most people, your books will show up here by default. Click on your name beneath one of your books.

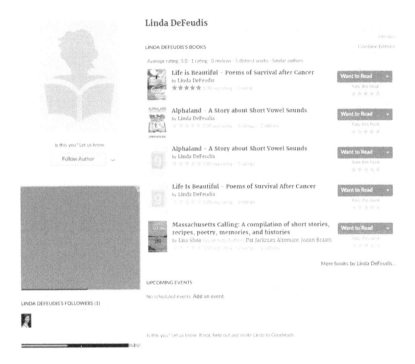

You'll note that this author profile is SEPARATE FROM your personal profile. They are two separate things. This author profile is not yet "claimed" even though you, the person, have a profile. That's because there could easily be many people with the same name out there. Goodreads wants to make sure they match the right name with the right books.

So in this case, Linda DeFeudis the person is indeed the same person as Linda DeFeudis the author. See the link at the very bottom? Where it says: "Is this you? Let us know."

Click on that.

BECOMING A GOODREADS AUTHOR

Goodreads is going to want to confirm you really are the author of these books.

Join the Goodreads Author Program

Are you Linda DeFeudis, author of the books below?

About the Author Program
Authors on Goodreads
Author Guidelines
Author Program How-To
Author Newsletter Archive
Ask the Author: Featured Authors
About Goodreads

To claim your profile to promote your work, please provide the following information:

- Your email address.
- Email address of your most recent publisher or agent.
- If self-published, indicate "Self-Published Author."
- If some titles listed are not yours, please list each book that is not yours. Alternatively, join the Goodreads Librarians Group and provide them with a link and the necessary information for separating the incorrect titles.
- Link to external website of all your published books, if available.
- Link to your Twitter or Facebook page, if available.

By submitting my application, I verify that the information provided is correct and that the profile I'm claiming on Goodreads is my own.

Submit Application

Put in whatever you can to confirm this information. Don't stress too much about what you put in. A real human reads this to confirm you are who you say you are.

You'll get a confirmation page just letting you know this could take a day or two to set up.

Thanks for your application! We'll review the information and will alert you via email when your application ✕ has been approved.

Please Note: If you have multiple pen names, you must claim each author profile using a unique Goodreads account with a unique email address. Read more here.

The Goodreads Author Program

BECOME A GOODREADS AUTHOR   **Goodreads Author**

Any author, anywhere in the world, can join the Goodreads Author Program for free. All you need is an Internet connection and a published book (or a soon-to-be published book) that can be found in our database. The Goodreads Author Program allows published authors to claim their profile page to promote their book and engage with readers. Once verified, your author profile will include the official Goodreads Author badge, which you can use to tell your fans to follow you on Goodreads.

Benefits of Claiming Your Profile Page

MANAGE YOUR PROFILE

Update your profile picture, write your bio, and fix your book listings—by joining the Goodreads Author Program you're able to keep the information about yourself up-to-date.

PROMOTE YOUR BOOKS

Run a giveaway, connect your blog, advertise your books—the Goodreads Author Program gives you access to the marketing tools you need to build buzz around your books.

INTERACT WITH READERS

Take questions from readers using Ask The Author, write reviews, and show off your taste in literature. Readers love to learn what books their favorite authors are reading!

CLAIM YOUR PROFILE TODAY

Follow these steps to apply for the Author Program:

1. Sign in or create an account, and then search for your most popular book via ISBN, ASIN, or title.
2. On the book, click on your author name. Scroll to the bottom of your author profile page.
3. Click "Is this you? Let us know!" to complete and submit the application.

We will send you an email when you're approved within 2 business days. Your login and password will stay the same.

Already a Goodreads Author? Learn how to use the Author Program effectively on our Authors & Advertisers Blog.

View All Goodreads Authors
Ask The Author
Authors & Advertisers Blog
Author Guidelines
Author Program Resources
Author Program FAQ
About Goodreads
Jobs
Blog
Press
Contact
Advertisers
Author Program
API
Librarian Manual
Help
Follow Goodreads on Twitter
Follow Goodreads on Facebook

That's all right. In the meantime, let's look at the other areas of Goodreads and get going.

CHAPTER 3 – GROUPS

A key way to draw attention to your projects is to post in various groups. Groups are the lifeblood of the Goodreads system.

Let's learn more about how they work.

FINDING GROUPS

Groups are the main method of interaction on Goodreads. There are literally thousands of groups out there on all sorts of topics.

To find groups, click on Community – Groups in the top menu bar.

CHOOSING GROUPS

It's fine to sign up for a bunch of groups as you get started. It lets you test the waters. See which you like the most. So search on topics you like. Poetry. SciFi. Mystery. Whatever it is that interests you.

So in this case I searched on Poetry.

Groups > Search

Find Groups by Title or Description   Search

showing 1-10 of 7391   sort by last activity ▼

All About Books — 3786 members — Last Activity 8 minutes ago
Books & Literature   • General
We're here because we like reading and we like chatting about reading. But we are here especially because we strongly believe that reading is not just ...more

For Love of a Book — 1605 members — Last Activity 8 minutes ago
Books & Literature   • Literature & Fiction
This group was created to connect lovers of stories across the internet with their characters and plotlines, dreams and recommendations. Bibliophiles ...more

House of LitnLife — 54 members — Last Activity 16 minutes ago
Books & Literature   • Literature & Fiction
This is a small community of readers devoted to reading primarily 19th century British and European classics. Recently, we read The Way We Live Now. P ...more

The Read Around The World Book Club — 38 members — Last Activity 17 minutes ago
Books & Literature   • Literature & Fiction
I have created this book club to read books from all over the world, mainly from female authors or from marginalized groups within countries.

We will ...more

Weekly Short Stories Contest and Company! — 973 members — Last Activity 23 minutes ago
Books & Literature   • General
Each week we have a different contest in both short stories and poetry and a poll to see who wins after each contest. No prizes except a chance to be ...more

Pick-a-Shelf — 1434 members — Last Activity 23 minutes ago
Just for Fun   • Too Much Information
The purpose to this group is to challenge all you avid readers out there to expand your reading beyond your preferred genres. Who knows you may find s ...more

You can see, for each group, how many members they have and how active they are. Generally it's best to choose groups with a large number of members and which are active. That gives you the best attention for the posts you make

When you click on a group you'll get more details about it. Its member count. Its moderators. You'll see the types of posts made there.

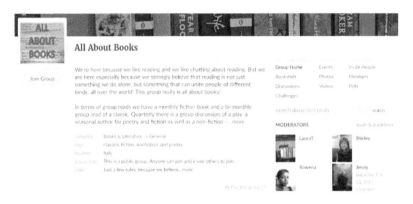

You'll have the option to "join group" beneath its main icon. It's fine to join a variety of groups at first, to see what they're like. You can always leave them later if you wish.

When you join a group, you have options about how you want to get updates. I always opt to not get any updates. It helps avoid the email deluge.

All About Books > **Join Group**

Do you want to join the group All About Books?

group discussion email settings

○ **Digest** - Get all comments on group discussions bundled in a daily or weekly email (the frequency is configured on your 'account settings' page).

○ **Individual Email** - Get an email instantly when someone starts a new topic in this group, and whenever someone replies. You will not get a second notification email about a topic until you've visited the discussion. *Warning, for larger groups, this could get a little bit out of control!*

○ **Notification only** - Don't get any emails, just get notifications on your homepage of new discussion comments in this group.

○ **None** - Do not get any notifications about group discussions. You can change this later on the 'my account' page.

Join Group   Cancel

That's it! You've now joined the group.

POSTING IN A GROUP

Be sure to read through a few threads in a group before posting. That will give you a sense about what the group is like.

Make an introductory post saying hello to the group. That's always a good way to start. Do NOT be heavy on marketing here. Groups are sensitive about people using them just to blast out promotions. Talk about yourself mostly at first.

Then make a gentle post or two in a few of their threads, adding to the discussion.

See how other authors or promoters use the forums. Wait a few days before doing anything promotional.

FREEBIE GROUPS

Make sure you do searches on words like "freebies", "giveaways", and so on. Join a few of those groups. Not only will you learn about books you can get for free yourself, but you'll build a network of places to market your own efforts.

These groups can often get heavy traffic and they're perfect places to promote your own books.

REVIEW GROUPS

There are many groups out there that offer reviews. These are both generic review groups and also topic-specific groups, like cozy mystery, which have a review area.

Look through the groups to find areas which suit your needs. Pretty much every author could use more reviews. These groups are how you find interested individuals.

CHAPTER 4 – GETTING IMAGES READY TO POST

There will be times on Goodreads that you'll want to post images. Maybe it's the image of your latest author signing. Maybe it's an image of your new product.

While you can certainly post raw photos right out of your camera or phone, it's worthwhile to do a bit of editing to the image. That way you put your best foot forward in the marketing of your brand.

TAKE A HIGH QUALITY PHOTO

Twitter is a very visual system. And while lots of people use Twitter on their small smartphones, many people do use Twitter on large-screen computers. They will be able to appreciate the fine detail on the higher quality image. They will be far more likely to like and remember that image. It's well worth it for you to give them that high quality image if at all possible.

That means, then, having a camera that can take photos of that pixels level or larger.

Yes, many smartphones have that ability, but in many cases you'll want to be able to adjust the aperture to create a soft, fuzzy background. That lets the viewer focus on the main aspect of the image.

Lisa Shea

Perhaps you'll want to be able to adjust the shutter speed to capture motion just right.

These are often tasks handled with great precision by larger-sized cameras with more specialized controls and larger lenses. Especially if you are aiming to sell a product or entice someone with a book cover, you want to ensure that image is as perfect as possible.

A good camera doesn't have to be incredibly expensive. If you do your research you can find one that has the controls you need within your budget, especially if you look on eBay or other similar sites.

Also, try talking with local camera clubs. Maybe you can work with someone there and have them take some photos for you in exchange for something.

If the item you're taking a photo of *is* a piece of art, like a watercolor painting or a sculpture, there are entire books and classes on how to do that well. Do some web research to start. It's critical you use proper lighting and setup to get everything to represent well on the JPG / RAW file version.

However you do it, getting those high quality photos is a key first step. Twitter is quite attentive to professional image, since it is primarily about jobs and marketing. If you have a low quality, poorly lit, fuzzy image, it will harm you rather than help you.

ENHANCING THE PHOTO

Sure, master photographers can take the one perfect photo, have it cropped perfectly, and go with that without touching. However, for the rest of us we need to do some tweaking.

I use Photoshop myself. I have friends who use Lightroom and other programs. Find a program that works well for you and learn all of its abilities. You might be amazed at how subtle changes in contrast and light balance can really make a photo or image pop.

It's worth it to at least take a run at it in your editing program of choice to see if you can improve the image. Remember, once you post it, this will represent you and your brand. If you're an author it might not be the end of the world if your book cover is slightly dark – but if you're an artist, that's your end product there on the screen.

STORING THE PHOTO

Always, always, always store a copy of your photo on your local system or your cloud account. Don't just have it on your phone! Phones get lost, dropped, stolen, you name it. Always keep backups.

It's a good idea to develop a storage organization system that works for you. Many people do it by date and then subject within the dates.

Whatever you do, stick with it. Don't just toss photos into random folders. You never know when you'll need one of those photos.

Also, back up regularly. I have one friend who keeps backup drives in a local safe deposit box. Photos are irreplaceable. You always want access to those original, full size images.

When you're ready to save the Twitter version, give it a name that indicates that. So perhaps Marigold-TW.jpg. That would be the final version. Never destroy that original file – you might want to use it again some other time.

Now that the image is ready, you're able to post!

CHAPTER 5 – GIVEAWAYS

If you're an author, a giveaway is a powerful way to get attention for your book. If you're not an author, signing up for giveaways are great ways to get a pile of free things sent to you. So, either way, it's good to know how giveaways work.

GIVEAWAY LISTINGS

To view the existing giveaways, click on Browse, and the
Giveaways.

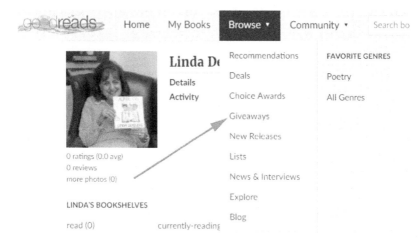

You'll see right there a list of all giveaways running. By
default it shows you the ones about to expire, but you have a
variety of sorting options.

When you choose to enter a giveaway, you're asked to enter
your address for the prize to be sent to:

Enter Giveaway

Enter for a chance to win

This book giveaway is open to members in the following countries: US, CA, GB, and AU.

Entry period begins on Mar 24, 2017 and ends on May 24, 2017

The author or publisher listing the giveaway is the sponsor, and if you win, they will receive your shipping address and they are responsible for shipping you the book. Goodreads is not a sponsor of the giveaway.

enter your shipping address

Full Name	Linda DeFeudis	Please use your real name to ensure delivery
Company name		Company, c/o
Address Line 1		Street address, P.O. box
Address Line 2		Apartment, suite, unit, building, floor, etc.
City		
State/Province/Region		
ZIP/Postal Code		
Country	United States ▼	

Add Address

Don't worry about spam here. This is a legal requirement and I've never been spammed by Goodreads. This is just one of those legal things to make sure you're a valid entry. It's also to ensure that people don't just spam-enter every single giveaway with the click of one button. At least people had to type in information to make their entry.

Enter a few giveaways. See how this works. It will help you understand, if you're an author, how you should set up your own promotional text to best catch the eye.

If you win a book, be sure to thank the author! And consider leaving a review for it as well.

CHAPTER 6 - BUILDING AN AUTHOR ACCOUNT

Once Goodreads approves your author account, they will send you an email. Usually that takes around 1-2 days depending on how busy they are.

When your author account is approved, it's time to get to work. This author account is how you manage your books, build your followers, and spread the news about your efforts.

AUTHOR DASHBOARD

Here is what the author dashboard looks like. This is your main page for your author account:

Your dashboard has your name and photo, a list of all books the system knows about, and options to do a variety of things. You can add in another book. Edit your profile. Answer questions. Build followers.

Let's get started!

ADDING A BOOK

Because Goodreads is now owned by Amazon, pretty much any book that is in Amazon should show up in Goodreads within a week or two. When you create a new book on Amazon, I recommend being patient and allowing that process to happen. Otherwise, if you add the book, and then Amazon auto-adds the same book, you've got two books that you have to merge together.

Still, if you wait a few weeks and the book still doesn't appear in Goodreads, there's a system to add the book in manually. That link is "Add a book" on the top right of your dashboard page.

Author Dashboard

Check the stats for your books and giveaways, and learn more about how to promote your books on Goodreads.

My Author Profile »
Edit My Author Profile »
Add a book »

Linda DeFeudis's Stats

Linda DeFeudis's Stats
★★★★★ 5.00 avg rating — 1 rating

number of works	3	added by unique users	1
total books added	3	followers	1
total ratings	1	friends	0
total reviews	0	books I've added	0
on to-read shelf	0	books I've reviewed	0

View recent work stats »

AUTHORS & ADVERTISERS

Stay updated about new prod
case studies for authors.

Summer Reading for Autho
Marketing

Summer is just around the cor
which means you'll hopefully
done. You can tell readers via

When you click that, you get an entry screen with a variety of forms. You enter the title, description, format, number of pages, and other items. It's ok to leave some fields blank, like publisher and edition. It's mostly key that you have the title, description, format, and a cover image.

Add a New Book

Add a cover image for this book.
Choose File | No file chosen

Note: Goodreads has over 12 million books in its database already, so please do a search before adding a book, as it may be a duplicate. Please also carefully read the guidelines to the right, especially the part about what kind of books to add.

Guidelines

- **Authors:** Add authors in the order they are listed on the book cover, or alphabetically if there is no cover or various editions disagree.
- **Format:** Should generally be Hardcover, Paperback, Audio CD, Ebook, etc.
- **Title:** If the book is in a series, put which book it is in parenthesis after the title. For example: Harry Potter and the Sorcerer's Stone (Harry Potter, #1). More rules are here.
- **Types of books:** Please only add books. Books generally have ISBN numbers (but don't have to), and are usually published. Periodicals such as newspapers, magazines, and comics are not books. However a volume of comics or articles or a graphic novel is considered a book.

For more tips please read the Librarian Manual.

title *	
sort by title *	
author *	Linda DeFeudis Add Role
	Add new author
isbn	isbn 13 Click for ASIN
publisher	
published	year month: ▼ day: ▼
number of pages	
format	▼ Other
edition	
description	

edition language	Select ▼

Once you submit this form, it can take 15 minutes or so for it to fully get into the system. And then you're set! The book is now part of Goodreads. You can edit these later so don't worry about it being exactly perfect the first time.

DIFFERENT EDITIONS / COVERS FOR A BOOK

This often confuses people new to Goodreads so it's important to understand how this works.

Goodreads tracks a different entry for each edition or cover for a given book. You never "change" a book's cover in Goodreads. You always add a new edition with the new cover. This is because many readers want their Goodreads entry to match the book they have on their shelves. It makes it easier for that reader to find the book. So if your book has three different covers, there are going to be three different editions for that book in Goodreads. They are all connected together, but there are still different entries for them.

When you want to add a new cover for your book, you don't change that existing cover. You add a new edition with the new cover.

So let's take a look at Linda's current listing of books.

Books by Linda DeFeudis

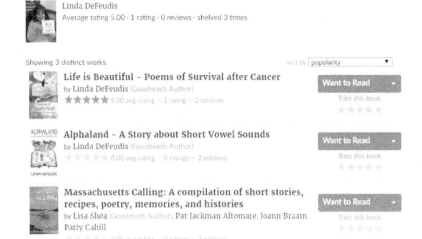

Linda DeFeudis
Average rating 5.00 · 1 rating · 0 reviews · shelved 3 times

Showing 3 distinct works.   sort by   popularity ▼

Life is Beautiful - Poems of Survival after Cancer
by Linda DeFeudis (Goodreads Author)
★★★★★ 5.00 avg rating — 1 rating — 2 editions

Want to Read ▾
Rate this book
★★★★★

ALPHALAND **Alphaland - A Story about Short Vowel Sounds**
by Linda DeFeudis (Goodreads Author)
★★★★★ 0.00 avg rating — 0 ratings — 3 editions

Want to Read ▾
Rate this book
★★★★★

Massachusetts Calling: A compilation of short stories, recipes, poetry, memories, and histories
by Lisa Shea (Goodreads Author), Pat Jackman Altomare, Joann Braam, Patty Cahill
★★★★★ 0.00 avg rating — 0 ratings — 2 editions

Want to Read ▾
Rate this book
★★★★★

* Note: these are all the books on Goodreads for this author. To add more books, click here.

See how Alphaland says it has 3 editions out? If you click on Alphaland you can see those three distinct editions.

So it has the main current edition and then other editions. In this case there is a Kindle (ebook) edition, a paperback black-and-white edition, and a paperback color edition. They're all the same book, just different versions.

Here's another example so you can see how this works with different covers.

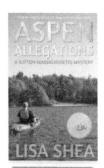

Want to Read

Rate this book

★ ★ ★ ★ ★

Read Book* Different edition

Aspen Allegations (Sutton Massachusetts Mystery #1)

by Lisa Shea (Goodreads Author)

★ ★ ★ ★ ★ 3.61   Rating Details · 165 Ratings · 45 Reviews

A ROMANTIC YOGA MYSTERY INFUSED BY NATURE

Morgan has become settled in her quiet life in Sutton, Massachusetts. Her peaceful morning yoga routine is assisted by her cat, Juliet. In the evening she guides her kayak across the placid surface of Lake Singletary. Everything is in its place.

When Morgan stumbles across a dead body in the shadowy depths of Sutton Woods, her stabil ...more

Paperback, 300 pages
Published March 6th 2013 by Minerva Webworks LLC
(first published March 1st 2013)

Series	Sutton Massachusetts Mystery #1
Literary Awards	Independent Publisher Book Award (IPPY) (2013)
Other Editions (12)	

All Editions | Add a New Edition | Combine

So this one has 13 different editions – the primary one and the 12 alternatives. The other twelve are different covers and different formats.

COMBINING EDITIONS INTO A BOOK

Sometimes something goes awry with Goodreads and they don't properly combine your editions together into a single book. You can manage that yourself.

On your main dashboard, go to your book list. On that book list, on the right side, is the link to combine editions.

On this page you can combine editions. You can also separate them out again, if something gets mis-combined.

Linda DeFeudis > Combine Editions

On this page you can combine different editions of the same book. This way all reviews and ratings will apply to all editions of the book.

Only combine books you are sure are editions of the same work.
Only combine editions of a single work at a time.

| Combine Editions | auto-combine | filter works by keyword | Filter Works |

☐ **Alphaland - A Story about Short Vowel Sounds**
   Alphaland - A Story about Short Vowel Sounds (Paperback) details | edit | separate
   Alphaland - A Story about Short Vowel Sounds (Full Color Version) (Paperback) details | edit | separate
   Alphaland - A Story about Short Vowel Sounds (Kindle Edition) details | edit | separate

separate tool

☐ **Life is Beautiful - Poems of Survival after Cancer**
   Life is Beautiful - Poems of Survival after Cancer (Kindle Edition) details | edit | separate
   Life Is Beautiful - Poems of Survival After Cancer (Paperback) details | edit | separate

separate tool

| Combine Editions |

The above view is correct. You want one entry for each book, with all the editions gathered together for that book.

SERIES

If you have a series of books, that is listed at the lower part of your author dashboard page.

SERIES BY LISA SHEA

The Sword of Glastonbury
(14 books)
by Lisa Shea (Goodreads Author)
★★★★ 3.72 avg rating — 971 ratings

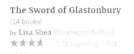

Black Cat (31 books)
by Lisa Shea (Goodreads Author)
★★★★ 2.65 avg rating — 274 ratings

A Regency Time Travel Romance (3 books)
by Lisa Shea (Goodreads Author)
★★★★ 3.41 avg rating — 395 ratings

Sutton Massachusetts Mystery (4 books)
by Lisa Shea (Goodreads Author)
★★★★ 3.69 avg rating — 186 ratings

Journaling Prompts (9 books)
by Lisa Shea (Goodreads Author)
★★★★ 3.54 avg rating — 196 ratings

More series by Lisa Shea...

When you click on a given series, you see all the books in that series.

Sutton Massachusetts Mystery series

4 works, 4 primary works

A series of mystery novels set in Sutton, Massachusetts.

All novels in the Sutton Massachusetts Mystery series are written in a boots-on-the-ground, chapter-a-day format. Author Lisa Shea goes to the locations, experiences the atmosphere, and then infuses those colors, birdsongs, and fragrances into her story in a manner reminiscent of Annie Dillard's Pilgrim at Tinker Creek.

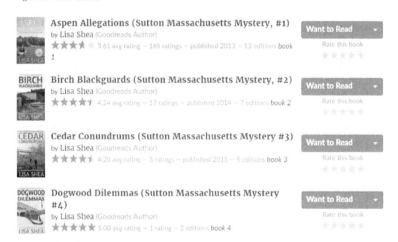

Aspen Allegations (Sutton Massachusetts Mystery, #1)
by Lisa Shea (Goodreads Author)
★★★★ 3.61 avg rating — 165 ratings — published 2013 — 13 editions book 1

Want to Read
Rate this book

Birch Blackguards (Sutton Massachusetts Mystery, #2)
by Lisa Shea (Goodreads Author)
★★★★ 4.24 avg rating — 17 ratings — published 2014 — 7 editions book 2

Want to Read
Rate this book

Cedar Conundrums (Sutton Massachusetts Mystery #3)
by Lisa Shea (Goodreads Author)
★★★★ 4.20 avg rating — 5 ratings — published 2015 — 5 editions book 3

Want to Read
Rate this book

Dogwood Dilemmas (Sutton Massachusetts Mystery #4)
by Lisa Shea (Goodreads Author)
★★★★★ 5.00 avg rating — 1 rating — 2 editions book 4

Want to Read
Rate this book

You can't create series by yourself. This is something the Goodreads librarians do.

First, go to the groups listing and search on the Goodreads Librarians Group. Join it.

Now scroll down to the area called "Serieses!" Make a post there telling them which of your books need to be put together into a series, and the name of that series.

Within a few hours your series should be created for you.

ASK THE AUTHOR

Goodreads lets readers ask you questions. This is a great way to build traffic and interest for your site.

The area for this is in the middle of your author dashboard.

ASK THE AUTHOR   Learn more

My Ask the Author Settings

Allow Goodreads members to ask you questions   ● On   ○ Off

Question Digest Emails   ○ None ● Daily ○ Weekly

Update my Message to Readers

You can customize this message for your readers! For example: "I'll be answering questions about my new book this week." or "I'll be answering one question per week in September."

Pending Questions (6)

g   Goodreads a moment ago   Answer · Skip
    Where did you get the idea for your most recent book?

g   Goodreads a moment ago   Answer · Skip
    How do you get inspired to write?

g   Goodreads a moment ago   Answer · Skip
    What are you currently working on?

g   Goodreads a moment ago   Answer · Skip
    What's your advice for aspiring writers?

g   Goodreads a moment ago   Answer · Skip
    What's the best thing about being a writer?

g   Goodreads a moment ago   Answer · Skip
    How do you deal with writer's block?

                                            View Answered Questions

You can turn the option on and off easily. Once it's on, answer a few questions! If there's a particular question you'd like to talk about, get a friend of yours to "ask" it on your page so you can then answer it.

GOODREADS BLOG

I highly recommend having a blog on Goodreads. It's a great way to remind your fans about what you're up to.

You can post directly into Goodreads or you can connect to a RSS feed from WordPress or other systems.

YOUR BLOG

You have not created a blog yet. Your author profile has 1 follower which will be subscribed to your blog if you do. Creating a blog is a great way to collect followers, and each time you blog your followers will see your post on their home pages.

start a blog

Whichever way you do it, make sure you check weekly for responses. That way if people comment on your blog post you can respond to them.

I personally use a RSS feed from WordPress. That way when I post to WordPress it makes a matching post here on Goodreads. As an added bonus, each post on Goodreads encourages people to go visit my LisaShea.com site for more information.

May 22, 2017

Evening meditation time

Evening meditation time. It might sound illogical, but taking a short break to regain focus actually makes everything go more quickly. You don't lose the time – you gain time overall. #namaste

The post Evening meditation time appeared first on Lisa Shea Blog.

View more on Lisa Shea's website »

Like · 0 comments ·
flag

Published on May 22, 2017 19:00 · 2 views

new book on Self-Publishing

I'm finalizing my new book on Self-Publishing – it covers the process on Kindle, iTunes, CreateSpace, Kobo, and more. Any thoughts on the cover? Let me know! I'll let you know when I'm ready for beta-readers :).

The post new book on Self-Publishing appeared first on Lisa Shea Blog.

View more on Lisa Shea's website »

Like · 0 comments · flag

RUNNING A GIVEAWAY

Giveaways are only for paperback copies of books. If you have paperback books, consider running a giveaway. It's a great way to get thousands of people to know about your book. Even if those people don't win it, they might end up buying it.

The link to create a giveaway is at the lower section of your Goodreads author dashboard.

YOUR GIVEAWAYS

Listing a giveaway is a great way to get free exposure for your book! You can list any of your pre-release or published books for a giveaway, regardless of publication date.

It's best to set up your giveaway at least 7 to 10 days in advance to allow for approval and any last-minute edits, but you can set up a giveaway up to 3 months in advance if you like! We recommend running your giveaway for 1 month to maximize entries. This allows the giveaway enough time to generate buzz.

You have not listed any book giveaways. List one now.

Make sure your book is wholly set up with the cover and description you want before you start the Goodreads giveaway process.

It'll take a while for their admin to do the setup, so plan ahead for these. Also, read through a number of the existing giveaways to get a sense of what types of promotional texts work best.

I recommend doing US-only first. The shipping prices to non-US locations can get fairly high.

Once the giveaway is set up, be sure to publicize it. Send links out on your newsletter, on Facebook, on Twitter, and so on. This is a great way to drum up interest in your book.

Giveaways used to be completely free to run. Now that Amazon owns Goodreads, suddenly authors are being charged quite a lot of money to run giveaways. So you'll want to see how this works in your budget.

CHAPTER 7 – LISTS

Some people never use lists at all. Other people swear by lists.

Just what are lists and how are they useful for authors?

LIST BASICS

Lists are collections of books on a given topic. Best science fiction books of all time. Best cozy mysteries set in Maine. If you can get your book onto a list, it means people who are interested in that topic will find and hopefully read your book.

Note that lots of people on Goodreads never use lists at all. Still, it's good to reach every person you can with your efforts.

The list of lists is here:

https://www.goodreads.com/list

You can see that readers can add books into a list. They can also vote on existing books on a list.

FINDING A LIST

You can use the 'search' feature in the list area to find books on a given topic. Let's say you're looking for books which feature a hero or heroine in the Autism spectrum. You could search the lists on autism and find:

https://www.goodreads.com/list/show/72065.Books_Featuring_Children_and_Teens_with_Autism

Yup, this list showcases books with a hero or heroine with autism.

To add a new book to that list, there's a button right at the top –

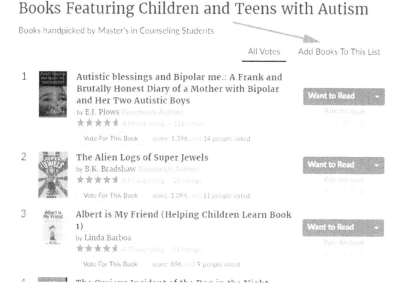

Now type in the title of the book you want to add, and vote to add it in.

Books Featuring Children and Teens with Autism

Books handpicked by Master's in Counseling Students

All Votes   Add Books To This List

Add books from: My Books or a Search

shelf all ▼   normal citizen   search my books
                                                 Books matching: normal citizen

Normal Citizen: The Fight For Justice   Vote For This Book
by Tom Brooks
shelf: read

If it's your own book, you'll want to ask a friend or family member to add your book to that list. You can't add or vote on your own books.

Once books are on a list, you can then ask family and friends to vote for the book. This is a good reason to build up your following on Goodreads. The more supporters you have, the more votes you can acquire. Your aim of course is to end up high on the list.

Still, if it's a relatively small list, just being on it helps a lot.

CREATING A LIST

If there's a topic you're interested in that doesn't have a list yet, why not create it? Just start at the list page –

https://www.goodreads.com/list

Do a search first to make sure the list really doesn't exist. Maybe you love books set in Worcester, Massachusetts. There isn't a list for that. So click on "Create New List" in the top right to get started!

Fill in the fields with meaningful information. Remember, you want to be found in searches. So I would put:

Title:

Worcester Massachusetts Stories

Description:

Books, both fiction and non-fiction, set in the lovely city of Worcester Massachusetts. Mystery, romance, literary, sci-fi, horror - they're all game!

Key Words:

Worcester Massachusetts

Now enlist a few friends to add in your books and vote on them, and of course include other peoples' books which match the criteria.

Worcester Massachusetts Stories

Books, both fiction and non-fiction, set in the lovely city of Worcester Massachusetts. Mystery, romance, literary, sci-fi, horror - they're all game!

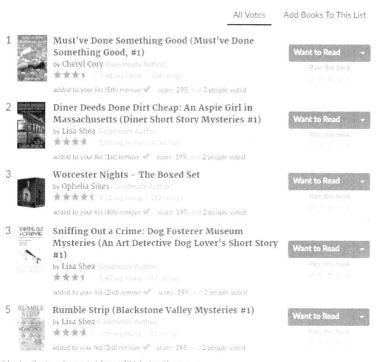

All Votes   Add Books To This List

1   **Must've Done Something Good (Must've Done Something Good, #1)**
    by Cheryl Cory (Goodreads Author)
    ★★★½   3.48 avg rating — 324 ratings
    added to your list (5th) remove ✔   score: 295, and 3 people voted

    Want to Read
    Rate this book

2   **Diner Deeds Done Dirt Cheap: An Aspie Girl in Massachusetts (Diner Short Story Mysteries #1)**
    by Lisa Shea (Goodreads Author)
    ★★★½   3.86 avg rating — 43 ratings
    added to your list (1st) remove ✔   score: 199, and 2 people voted

    Want to Read
    Rate this book

3   **Worcester Nights - The Boxed Set**
    by Ophelia Sikes (Goodreads Author)
    ★★★★½   4.12 avg rating — 152 ratings
    added to your list (4th) remove ✔   score: 197, and 2 people voted

    Want to Read
    Rate this book

3   **Sniffing Out a Crime: Dog Fosterer Museum Mysteries (An Art Detective Dog Lover's Short Story #1)**
    by Lisa Shea (Goodreads Author)
    ★★★½   3.40 avg rating — 47 ratings
    added to your list (2nd) remove ✔   score: 197, and 2 people voted

    Want to Read
    Rate this book

5   **Rumble Strip (Blackstone Valley Mysteries #1)**
    by Lisa Shea (Goodreads Author)
    ★★★½   3.56 avg rating — 18 ratings
    added to your list (3rd) remove ✔   score: 195, and 2 people voted

    Want to Read
    Rate this book

5 books · 2 voters · list created August 19th by Lisa Shea

Over time the list will grow and attract even more attention for our books.

You can help out fellow authors this way, of course. For example, a friend of mine, Tom Hollyday, writes mysteries set in the Chesapeake Bay. When I did a search I found an author had made up a list of mysteries in the Chesapeake Bay. Excellent! I promptly added Tom's eight books to this list.

WHAT LISTS ARE MY BOOK IN?

To figure out which lists your book is currently in, just go to the book's detail page. Scroll down.

In between the questions about your book and the community reviews will be the area where the lists are enumerated.

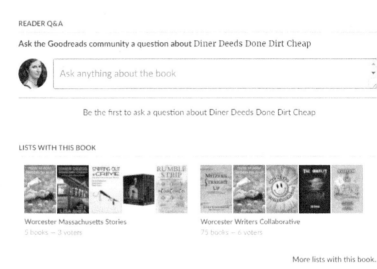

This can help you encourage voting on your book and to know if you should seek out more lists to get added onto.

CHAPTER 8 - CREATIVE WRTING

Goodreads is fostering an area very much like Wattpad – an area where people can post story ideas and get feedback on them.

That area is called "Creative Writing".

It's a good way to get your material to be found where there's less competition.

STARTING OUT IN CREATIVE WRITING

Begin by clicking on 'Community' in the top menu bar, then 'Creative Writing'.

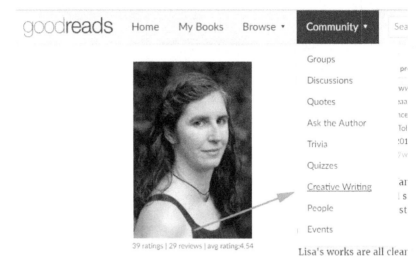

39 ratings | 29 reviews | avg rating:4.54

Lisa's works are all clear

Once there, you'll see all the current options sorted by categories. Some tags, like art, might have only a few entries while others, like love, might have thousands.

You can search on key words or browse by category.

But what you really want to do, of course, is load in your own.

LOADING YOUR CREATIVE WRITING

Start by clicking on the 'my writing' link in the top right of the
Creative Writing area.

If you're new to this area, you'll be prompted to 'Get Started'.

Now you're presented with a form to enter your story. This is a
great way to publicize an existing book – you enter the first
few pages of it and then encourage people to buy the entire
thing on whatever sites you're selling your book on.

Add My Writing

title of this work

this story contains explicit content not suitable for minors

description

cover image: Choose File   No file chosen

genre: Select ▼

tags (comma separated: poetry, romance, science fiction, humor, harry potter, etc)

isbn (optional — if this writing is an excerpt from or fan fiction based on a particular book)

email me when someone votes or comments on my story

chapter title

your writing (chapter 1)

ill in each field. The title should match the title of your book,
f this is a sample. The same for the description. Use the cover
mage for your book as well. If this is a standalone piece you
aven't published elsewhere yet, this is a good test process for
ou to create those three items.

:hoose your genre and tags to help you be found by the right
udience. Do your best to choose a category that matches your
vork.

'hen paste in the chapter title and book content.

Vhen you're done, publish! You can always edit.

Diner Deeds Done Dirt Cheap – Book 1 (edit)

by Lisa Shea

description   Willow likes her quiet routine. She edits books from her small apartment. She occasionally goes out to the local diner for a tuna melt. She enjoys living in Worcester. It's where the Worcester Lunch Car Company made diners from 1906 to 1957. And now she gets to enjoy one in all its vintage glory.

But her quiet, predictable evening at the diner is disturbed when four restaurant workers come in complaining about a theft. And her inquisitive mind soon notices something ...

* * *

Diner Deeds Done Dirt Cheap is the first book in the Diner Short Story Mysteries series. These short stories are about 15- ...more

tags   asperger-s, aspergers, autism, diner, diners, massachusetts, mystery, mystery-series, worcester

genre   Mystery & Thrillers

stats   Published on 2017-08-19

book   **Diner Deeds Done Dirt Cheap: an Aspie Girl in Massachusetts**

Book 1 (edit)

Chapter 1 — Updated Aug 19, 2017 — 18,048 characters

I count each step as I make my way through the light drizzle of the chill April night. Eighty-seven. Eighty-eight. Eighty-nine as I curve around the large, muddy puddle that has swelled on the cracked sidewalk. There's no reason that I count; it just seems right. I always do it when the occasional urge for human company drives me from my small apartment and out into the streets of Worcester, Massachusetts. And I know from experience that the trek from the top floor of my olive-green triple-decker to the well-kept Boulevard Diner on Shrewsbury Street is exactly six hundred and forty two steps. So there's still a distance to cover.

This can be a good way to expose a new audience to your works which might not otherwise hear of it.

CHAPTER 9 – MESSAGES

Messages are wholly separate from public posts. It's important to understand how messages work.

You can set your messages to auto-forward to your home email address if you wish. That way you don't have to constantly log into Goodreads to see if you have anything new to answer there.

MESSAGES BASICS

To get to your messages, click the envelope icon in the top right of any page.

The inbox works the way pretty much all online mail systems do. You can compose new messages, read existing messages, delete them, reply to them, and so on.

If you get swamped with messages from a group you belong to, remember you can change the frequency you get those updates. You can also completely turn them off.

CHAPTER 10 - ADVANCED TIPS

Practice with Goodreads every day. Get a sense of how the system works.

When you've got a handle on those basics, it's time to move on to a few advanced topics!

GROWING YOUR FRIEND LIST

The more friends you have in Goodreads, the more views you get on your posts and updates. It's easy to build thousands of fans and friends here.

First, click on the head in the top right of your main menu bar to get to the friends area.

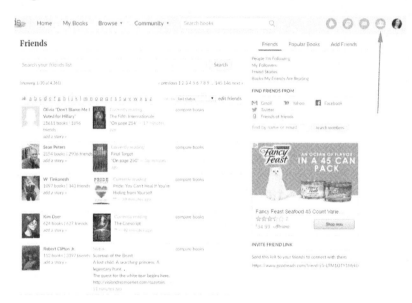

Use the 'find friends from' with Facebook and Twitter to suck in all of those friends. You can also use the 'friends of friends' while you only have a few. Once you cross 1,000 friends, this option turns off.

The more friends you build on Twitter and Facebook, the more friends you get here. The systems all support each other.

Encourage everyone you know to friend you on Goodreads. Likewise, make an effort to friend every author you know. Together we all support each other!

CHAPTER 11 – ISSUES TO AVOID

We've talked quite a lot about the ways to best use Goodreads. Now here's some advice about issues to watch out for.

DON'T ARGUE WITH REVIEWS

This is true on pretty much every system, but it's especially true here. Don't argue with reviews or reviewers. A reviewer is making their own personal statement about their emotions. They have a right to that. Especially keep in mind that Goodreads has its own peculiar way of handling stars. Re-read the section in the introduction of this book to remind yourself of how that works. A 2-star or 3-star review is actually pretty good.

If the reviewer makes a factual error, like claiming your book is full of sex when actually it's wholly clean without even a kiss, that is OK to make a gentle correction. Maybe the reviewer got mistaken between two different similar titles or something.

But other than that, let their point of view be. There are always going to be some people who dislike your book and that's fine. Those poor reviews help your overall review collection look more authentic. It looks more as if real humans are reviewing your book.

Then run some giveaways, do some marketing, and get a pile of better reviews to offset that negative one.

CHAPTER 12 - MULTIPLE GOODREADS ACCOUNTS

It is against Goodreads' rules to have multiple accounts for the same author name – and, really, there's no reason to do that.

That being said, you should create wholly separate accounts for each pen name. Log into each one with its own email address. Keep them entirely separate.

If you just have a few, it's fine to use separate browsers. That way you always use Chrome for User 1, IE for User 2, and so on. You don't have to log in and out that way. Each browser has its own cookies for each person.

CHAPTER 12 - LISA'S GOODREADS FEED

To get a sense of how I post, here is the link to my Goodreads feed:

https://www.goodreads.com/author/show/6432529.Lisa_Shea

Be sure to ask with any questions!

CHAPTER 13 - SUMMARY

Goodreads is a unique social network. It's primarily about readers and people who love books. It's especially important for authors to be available in this area – but it's also useful for other entrepreneurs to be here, chatting and spreading the word.

Best of luck to you, and contact me with any questions!

Thank you for reading this *Goodreads for Authors, Artists and Entrepreneurs* book! I hope you found some new tools which can help you in your marketing efforts.

If you found some of this information to be useful, please leave a review – I'd appreciate it immensely!

https://www.amazon.com/review/create-review?ie=UTF8&asin=B071PCN1RK

You can also post reviews on Goodreads and any other systems you use. Together we can help make a difference!

I support arts for children programs.

If you have a tip I didn't cover, please let me know! Together we can help each other build our skills.

SOCIAL MEDIA AUTHOR ESSENTIALS

Here are the books currently in my series on social media.
More are on their way!

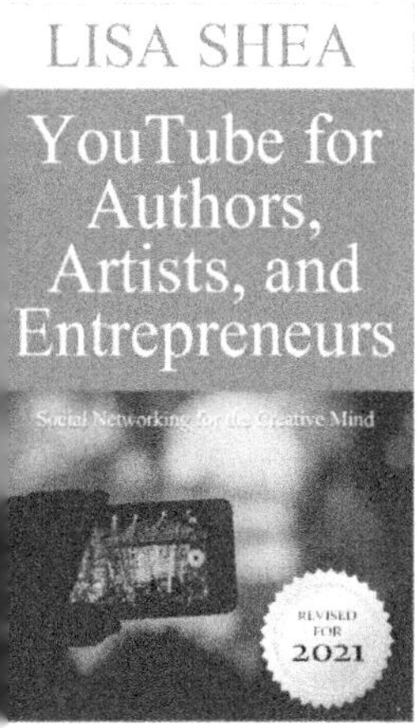
LISA SHEA
YouTube for Authors, Artists, and Entrepreneurs
Social Networking for the Creative Mind
REVISED FOR 2021

FREE EBOOKS

All of these books should be available for free from all platforms.

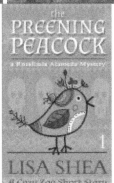

I may have added more free books since releasing this list here. For the most up to date version, be sure to visit:

http://www.lisashea.com/freebooks/

Thank you for supporting the cause!
Be the change you wish to see in the world.

DEDICATION

To the Boston Writer's Group, who supports me in all my projects.

My Sutton Writing Group is also quite helpful.

To my boyfriend, who encourages me in all of my dreams.

Most of all, to my loyal fans on GoodReads, Facebook, Twitter, and other systems who encourage me. Thank you so much for your enthusiasm!

GLOSSARY

Author account – a special ability granted to a standard account, to let an author manage their books.

Giveaways – contests where readers can win free books.

Goodreads– a social networking platform first launched in July 2006.

ABOUT THE AUTHOR

Lisa has always enjoyed helping others achieve their dreams in writing. She has owned BellaOnline for over fifteen years now. BellaOnline is a free training system for writers which teaches them everything from time management to clear writing to social networking. She publishes a quarterly literary magazine. She runs two separate writing groups to help both fiction and non-fiction authors achieve their goals.

One of Lisa's mantras is that we all help each other succeed. Authors are not in competition with each other. We are all here to elevate the selection of books available to our audience. Every voice deserves to be heard. Every author has a story to tell.

Together we all thrive!

A portion of my proceeds from my books benefit battered women's shelters.

Please visit the following pages for news about free books, discounted releases, and new launches. Feel free to post questions there – I strive to answer within a day!

Facebook:
https://www.facebook.com/LisaSheaAuthor

Twitter:
https://twitter.com/LisaSheaAuthor

GoodReads:
https://www.goodreads.com/lisashea/

Blog:
http://www.lisashea.com/lisabase/blog/

Newsletter:
http://www.lisashea.com/lisabase/subscribe.html

Share the news – we all want to enjoy interesting books!

Made in the USA
Las Vegas, NV
11 March 2022

45435710R00059